PENTABUS
RURAL THEATRE COMPANY

Pentabus Theatre Company and New Perspectives present

crossings

by **Deirdre Kinahan**

Crossings was commissioned by Pentabus and New Perspectives and first performed at Pentabus Theatre, Bromfield, Shropshire, on Wednesday 10 October 2018.

crossings

by **Deirdre Kinahan**

Cast

Victoria Brazier
Will O'Connell

Creative Team

Director	Sophie Motley
Set and Lighting Designer	Sarah Jane Shiels
Sound Designer	Helen Skiera
Costume and Props	Carl Davies
Movement Director	Kitty Winter
Voice and Accent Coach	Emma Stevens-Johnson
Associate Sound Designer	Joe Dines
Production Manager	Alison Willcox
Rehearsal Stage Manager	Chaz Webb
Touring Stage Manager	Ali Bakewell

Special thanks to:

Madeleine Bedford, Tim Brierley, David Gaukroger,
Talking Birds, The Courtyard Hereford, Sam Eccles,
Hereford Costume Store, Elizabeth Sanders and Adam Wall

Tour Dates 2018

Wednesday 10 October | 7.30 p.m. | Pentabus Theatre, Bromfield | Shropshire
Thursday 11 October | 7.30 p.m. | Pentabus Theatre, Bromfield | Shropshire
Friday 12 October | 7.30 p.m. | All Stretton Village Hall | Shropshire
Saturday 13 October | 7.30 p.m. | Ludlow Assembly Rooms | Shropshire

Tuesday 16 October | 6.00 p.m. | Hereford College of Arts | Herefordshire
Wednesday 17 October | 7.30 p.m. | Culmington Village Hall | Shropshire
Thursday 18 October | 7.30 p.m. | Quatt Village Hall | Shropshire

Thursday 25 October | 7.30 p.m. | Mansfield Old Library | Nottinghamshire
Friday 26 October | 7.30 p.m. | South Holland Centre, Spalding | Lincolnshire
Saturday 27 October | 7.30 p.m. | Geddington Village Hall | Northamptonshire

Tuesday 30 October | 7.30 p.m. | Theatre Severn, Shrewsbury | Shropshire
Wednesday 31 October | 7.30 p.m. | Worcester University | Worcestershire
Thursday 1 November | 7.30 p.m. | Leintwardine Centre | Herefordshire

Thursday 8 November | 7.30 p.m. | Thrumpton Village Hall | Nottinghamshire
Friday 9 November | 7.30 p.m. | Waingroves Community Association | Derbyshire
Saturday 10 November | 7.30 p.m. | South Luffenham Village Hall | Rutland

Wednesday 14 November | 7.30 p.m. | Blythe Bridge Care & Fun Club | Staffordshire
Thursday 15 November | 7.30 p.m. | Swythamley & Heaton Centre | Cheshire
Friday 16 November | 7.30 p.m. | Rutland County Museum | Rutland
Saturday 17 November | 7.30 p.m. | Biggin Village Hall | Derbyshire

Thursday 22 November | 7.30 p.m. | Lustleigh Village Hall | Devon
Friday 23 November | 7.30 p.m. | Durweston Village Hall | Dorset
Saturday 24 November | 7.30 p.m. | Toller Porcorum Village Hall | Dorset

CAST

VICTORIA BRAZIER

Recent theatre includes: *The Secret Garden* (York Theatre Royal/Theatre by the Lake); *Hard Times* (Northern Broadsides); *Tiny Heroes* (Daniel Bye); *Three Mothers* (Waterloo East); *Treasure Island, Beauty and the Beast, Oliver Twist* (The Dukes, Lancaster); *The Lost Boy* (Theatre in the Quarter); *The Snow Queen, The Borrowers* (New Vic); *Multi Story* (Monkeywood Theatre); *We're Not Going Back* (Red Ladder); *A Great War* (JB Shorts); *Charlotte's Web – The Musical* (Watershed Productions) and *Hobson's Choice* (Royal Exchange Theatre, Manchester).

Recent work for television and radio includes: *Emmerdale, Coronation Street* (ITV); *All at Sea* (CBBC); *Doctors* (BBC); *Craven* (Savvy for the BBC); *Heading Out* (Red Productions); *Ann Veronica, Jezebel, The Thrill of Love, New Grub Street* and *Home Front* (Radio 4).

WILL O'CONNELL

Will is a graduate of the Samuel Beckett Centre, Trinity College Dublin.

Recent theatre includes: *CLASS* (Traverse, Edinburgh/Galway Arts Festival/ Abbey/ Dublin Theatre Festival); *Swansong* (Kilkenny Arts Festival); *Luck Just Kissed You Hello* (HotForTheatre/GIAF/Dublin Theatre Festival); *Mother You* (Dublin Fringe/Louise White); *Way to Heaven* (Rough Magic Seeds); *Peer Gynt* (Rough Magic/Dublin Theatre Festival); *Moment, Hue and Cry* (Tall Tales); *Caligula* (Rough Magic Seeds/Dublin Theatre Festival); *Macbeth, King Lear, Hamlet* (Second Age); *The Hairy Ape* (Corcadorca); *Life Is A Dream* (Rough Magic) and *Julius Caesar* (Abbey). Will is Associate Artist with The Stomach Box Theatre Company and has performed in all their works to date, *Amnon and Tamar, A Season in Hell* and *No Worst There Is None* (Best Production – Irish Times Theatre Awards).

Recent work for film and television includes: *Little Women* (BBC/Playground); *Detainment* (Twelve Media); *Out of Innocence* (Defiant Films/Telegael); *Red Rock* (Element/TV3); *Moonfleet* (Sky); *Game of Thrones* (HBO) and *Parked* (Grand Pictures)

In addition to his acting, Will also works as a musician, singer and voiceover artist.

CREATIVE TEAM

DEIRDRE KINAHAN | WRITER
For Pentabus: *Crossings*.

Theatre includes: *Bé Carna* (Andrews Lane Theatre, Dublin Irish tour/ Edinburgh Fringe Festival); *Passage, Knocknashee* (also Irish tour); *Attaboy Mr Synge* (Civic, Dublin); *The Snow Child* (Ramor Theatre Cavan); *Maisy Daly's Rainbow* (Solstice Arts Centre); *Moment* (Project Arts Centre/Bush Theatre/ Irish tour/US & Canada tour); *Bogboy* (Project Arts Centre/Irish Arts Centre, New York/Irish tour); *Halcyon Days* – Edinburgh Fringe First winner (Dublin Theatre Festival/Irish tour/Irish Arts Centre, New York/Edinburgh Festival/ Warsaw); *Spinning* (Dublin Theatre Festival/Den, Chicago); *Wild Sky* (Rossnaree House, Meath/Bewley's Café Theatre, Dublin/Irish Arts Centre, New York/ Washington); *Rise* (The Old Vic); *Born, Me & Molly & Moo* (Meath County Council); *The Unmanageable Sisters, Rathmines Road* (Abbey, Dublin); *Wild Notes – The Frederick Douglas Project* (Solas Nua, Washington DC); *Lydia Glynn* (Manhattan Theatre Club, New York);

Short plays include: *Melody* (Site Specific Dublin/Irish tour/Òran Mór, Glasgow); *Hue & Cry* (Òran Mór, Glasgow/Bewleys Café Theatre, Dublin/ European tour); *The Fingers of Faverhsam, Transgressor* (Bush Theatre); *Broken* (Fishamble Theatre Company, Dublin/Sydney/Washington); *Protest* (Royal Court Theatre); *Renewed* (The Old Vic).

Radio plays include: *Bogboy* (RTÉ) and *The Bag on Ballyfinch Place* (BBC).

SOPHIE MOTLEY | DIRECTOR
Sophie grew up in South Shropshire and was based in Ireland from 2002 to 2016. She has directed four productions as Artistic Director of Pentabus: *Festival!, Here I Belong, Wolves Are Coming For You* and *New Futures*. Previously she was co-artistic director of WillFredd Theatre, Associate Director of Rough Magic in Dublin, Staff Director at English National Opera and Resident Assistant Director at the Abbey Theatre, Ireland's national theatre.

SARAH JANE SHIELS | SET AND LIGHTING DESIGNER

Sarah Jane began lighting design for Dublin Youth Theatre, completing a BA in Drama and Theatre Studies 2006 (Trinity), and the Rough Magic Seeds3 programme 2006–2008.

Lighting design includes: *FRNKNSTN* (Theatre Lovett); *Dolores, Soldier Still, Dusk Ahead* (Junk Ensemble); *Where We Live* (THISISPOPBABY); *East Belfast Boy/Every Day I Wake Up Hopeful* (Prime Cut); *Radio Rosario* (Little John Nee); *Jimmy's Hall, The Remains of Maise Duggan, Town is Dead* (Abbey, Dublin); *Dublin Oldschool* (Project Arts Centre); *The Effect, Everything Between Us, The Critic, The House Keeper, Plaza Suite* (Rough Magic); *PALS* – winner Irish Times Theatre Award Best Lighting 2015, *The Boys of Foley Street, Laundry, World's End Lane, Basin* (ANU Productions); *This Beach, Have I No Mouth, The Blue Boy, Silver Stars* (Brokentalkers).

Set and lighting design includes: *BEES!, Jockey, CARE, Farm, Follow* (WillFredd Theatre); *How to Keep an Alien* (Sonya Kelly/Rough Magic); *It Folds* – Winner Irish Times Theatre Award Best Lighting 2015 (Junk Ensemble/Brokentalkers).

HELEN SKIERA | SOUND DESIGNER

For Pentabus: *Crossings, Here I Belong.*

Theatre includes: *The Lovely Bones* (Royal & Derngate/tour); *This Is Not For You* (Graeae/Greenwich & Docklands International Festival/Stockton International Riverside Festival); *Instructions for Correct Assembly, Bodies* (Royal Court); *Betrayal, Echo's End, The Magna Carta Plays* (Salisbury Playhouse); *The Encounter* (Complicité); *Good Dog, I Know All The Secrets In My World, The Epic Adventure of Nhamo The Manyika Warrior and his Sexy Wife Chipo, The Legend of Hamba* (Tiata Fahodzi); *House and Garden* (Watermill); *Harajuku Girls* (Finborough); *The Dog, the Night, and the Knife, Pandora's Box, Sister Of, Miss Julie* (Arcola); *The Boy Who Climbed Out of His Face* (Shunt); *The Last Words You'll Hear* (Almeida at Latitude); *Advice for the Young at Heart* (Theatre Centre); *The Centre* (Islington Community Theatre); *The Three Sisters, The Laramie Project* (Guildhall School of Music & Drama); *Snow White, US/UK Exchange* (Old Vic New Voices); *Meat* (Bush Theatre); *Once In A Lifetime, The Eighth Continent, An Absolute Turkey* (E15); *Colors, The Criminals, House of Bones, Medea* (Drama Centre).

As Associate Sound Designer: *Barbershop Chronicles* (National Theatre); *Cat on a Hot Tin Roof* (Young Vic/Apollo); *Adler and Gibb* (Royal Court); *I'd Rather Goya Robbed Me of My Sleep Than Some Other Arsehole* (The Gate).

CARL DAVIES | COSTUME AND PROPS

Theatre includes: *A Brave Face, The Best Thing, Sharing Joy, Finding Joy, Nursing Lives* (Vamos Theatre); *Peggy's Song, For All I Care, Come Back Tomorrow* (National Theatre Wales); *Once Upon a Mattress, The Dreaming* (Lichfield Garrick); *The Eye of the Storm, It Will All be Over by Christmas* (Theatr Na-Nog); *The Boy, the Bee and the Blizzard* (Shoreditch Town Hall); *We are Lions Mr Manager* (Townsend Productions); *Looking through Glass, Alix In Wondergarthen* (Difficult Stage); *The Trials of Oscar Wilde, Still Life, Stage Beauty, Much Ado About Nothing, Dangerous Liaisons* (Mappa Mundi); *Belonging* (Re-Live); *Outlaw, Sleeping Beauty, Alice's Adventures, Road to Glory, Treasure Island, The Wind in the Willows, The Little Match Girl, The Snow Queen, A Christmas Carol, A Midsummer Night's Dream* (The Point, Eastleigh); *Oliver Twist, Oh no not Snow, Immune Nansi, Blodeuwedd* (Theatr Genedlaethol); *Lord of the Flies, Hansel and Gretel, James and the Giant Peach, The Jungle Book, Kes, The Borrowers* (The Courtyard).

KITTY WINTER | MOVEMENT DIRECTOR

Kitty Winter trained at Laban and Royal Central School of Speech and Drama.

For Pentabus: *Wolves are Coming for You, As the Crow Flies, Here I Belong.*

For New Perspectives: *Fisherman, Harvest.*

Recent movement credits include: *The Kite Runner* (Nottingham Playhouse/ Wyndham's/UK tour); *Peter Pan, Alice in Wonderland, Cinderella, A Christmas Carol, The Rise and Fall of Little Voice* (Derby Theatre); *Blood* (Tamasha/Belgrade Theatre Coventry); *Cinemusical, Cinemusical High* (Laurence Owen/Voodoo Rooms, Edinburgh); *Rapunzel, Jack, Tom's Midnight Garden* (Nottingham Playhouse); *Tiny Treasures, The Night Pirates* (Theatre Hullabaloo); *The Dog House, Puss in Boots, Women on the Verge of HRT* (Derby LIVE); *Roots* (Mercury Theatre Colchester); *Ghandi, Coconuts* (Kali/Arcola); *Dick Turpin's Last Ride* (Theatre Royal Bury St Edmunds).

Recent directing credits include: *Feet First, Car Story* (Box Clever); *Spinning Yarns, FIVE* (Theatre Hullabaloo/Theatre Direct, Canada); *Whose Shoes?* (Nottingham Playhouse); *Awaking Durga* (Kali/Soho).

For her own company WinterWalker Kitty has directed: *The Nutcracker and the Mouse King* (Watermans Arts Centre); *Three Keepers* (UK tour); *Come to the Circus* (Déda, Derby); *The Beast of Belper* (Belper Arts Festival).

EMMA STEVENS-JOHNSON | VOICE & ACCENT COACH

Emma Stevens-Johnson has worked within film and theatre for over 20 years. She began teaching accents in London in 2002. She has worked on international productions such as the critically acclaimed films *Submarine* and *Hellboy*; the new Netflix series *Apostle* and *Requiem* for the BBC. She has worked for BBC Cymru, S4C, BBC Radio and she is Voice Coach in Residence for Theatre Na n'Og. She has also worked for Theatre Royal Bath, Wales Millennium Theatre Company, Waking Exploits and Hijinx. Emma is a lecturer in Voice at The Royal Welsh College of Music and Drama. She has a Masters in Vocal Studies from Central School of Speech and Drama.

PENTABUS
RURAL THEATRE COMPANY

Pentabus is the nation's rural theatre company. We are the only professional theatre company in the UK whose vision is singularly rural. We tour new plays about the contemporary rural world to new audiences in village halls, fields, festivals and theatres, telling stories with local relevance and national impact. We believe that every person living in an isolated rural community has a right to exceptional theatre. We are based on a farm in Shropshire and all of our work is made here. It then tours village halls and theatres locally and nationally. Over four and a half decades we've produced 170 new plays, reached over 550,000 audience members, won a prestigious South Bank Show award for our show about racism, a Fringe First for our play about climate change and were the first to live stream from a village hall. We have hosted writers in residence since 2014; they have since been commissioned by the Royal Court, Birmingham Rep, Royal Welsh College and the Bush Theatre.

We are a champion for rural young people aged 16 to 25 and Pentabus Young Company is our new initiative offering workshops, masterclasses, work experience and mentorships, as well as the opportunity to join our Young Writers' Group, which has been running for five years. Our Young Writers' Groups have had their work presented at Ludlow Fringe, Latitude Festival and The Courtyard Hereford.

You can find out more about us at **www.pentabus.co.uk**

Twitter @pentabustheatre | Facebook Pentabus Theatre
Pentabus Theatre Company, Bromfield, Ludlow, Shropshire, SY8 2JU

Artistic Director	Sophie Motley
Managing Director	Kitty Ross
Managing Director (Maternity Cover)	Catrin John
Development Manager	Francesca Spickernell
Development Manager (Maternity Cover)	Verity Overs-Morrell
Producer	Jon Chartres
Audience Development & Engagement Manager	Andrew Sterry
Bookkeeper	Debbie Yapp
CSRC Writer-in-Residence	Sophie Ellerby
Associate Artists	Emma Dennis-Edwards & Tim Foley
Volunteers	Stephen Abbott, Mike Price & Ian Yarroll

Pentabus is a registered charity (number 287909). We rely on the generosity of our donors, small and large, to help us to make brilliant new theatre. We would like to thank all our supporters including:

Torchbearers: Richard Burbidge | Anne Haydock | Emma Kidson | David Lewis | Ros Robins | Hermoine Salwey | Neil Stuttard | Jenny Pearce | Diane Lennan | Joseph Motley | Derek Smith | David Thomas | Sue Thomas | Barbara Ann Tweedie
Beacons: James Mayor | Cecilia Motley | Mary Wells

Pentabus is also supported by the Clive & Sylvia Richards Charity, the Haystack Trust and The Millichope Foundation.

NEW PERSPECTIVES

New Perspectives is an East Midlands-based touring theatre company, specialising in bringing new work to rural and community audiences. Through an annual programme of original adaptations, rare revivals and new writing, we aim to bring live theatre that is vital, affordable and accessible into the heart of wide-ranging communities, as well as to regional, national and international venues.

Our work tours nationally and internationally, from small rural village halls to 700 seat theatres. Our mixed economy touring models enable us to tour and programme live performances in the heart of communities, affording opportunities for those with little or no access to other cultural outlets the opportunities to see high quality performances right on their doorstep. Removing barriers of location, age, culture or socio-economic status fuels our ambition to bring audiences into close contact with the highest quality new work.

We maintain the highest levels of artistry and production values in all our work, and deliver a programme of wide cultural significance and are therefore able to advance the arts through regular critical analysis of the work we create. Our productions are testament to the fact that rural theatre is as relevant, challenging and dynamic as theatre made for any other environment.

To find out more: **www.newperspectives.co.uk**

Twitter: NPtheatre | Facebook: newperspectivestheatrecompany |
Youtube: newperspectivesTV | Flickr: npimagegallery

New Perspectives is supported using funding by Arts Council England. As a registered charity No. 1053809 to find out how you might help to make a difference see **www.newperspectives.co.uk** or contact **Sally@newperspectives.co.uk**

CROSSINGS

Deirdre Kinahan

Characters

MARGARET
GRACE
SEAN
MIRJANA

This text went to press before the end of rehearsals and so may differ slightly from the play as performed.

ACT ONE

We are in a traditional English village hall. A piano sits in the corner.

The door opens and a woman, GRACE, *enters, it is spring 1919. She wears a fashionable suit, and hat with a veil, which covers her face. She holds a clutch bag and carries a box parcel tied with string. She looks around the room. She is expecting someone. She sits on a chair against the wall. She waits. She is awkward. She looks out the window. She then approaches the piano. She runs her hand along the piano, opens it up and hits a note. She puts her bag on top and starts to play the hymn 'Amazing Grace'… music first and then she sings… she has the voice of an Irishman.*

Another woman, MARGARET, *enters, she is unnoticed.* GRACE *moves effortlessly from the hymn to another tune 'Take Me Back to Dear Old Blighty'…* MARGARET *interrupts after a verse.*

MARGARET. Miss Doherty?

> GRACE *hits a discordant note and stops playing. She is a little aghast. She stands.*

GRACE. Yes. Yes. That's me. I'm. I am.

I am Miss Doherty.

They both stand in silence.

I… I just arrived.

On the train.

MARGARET. Very good.

GRACE. Yes. It is. It's very good. Very comfortable… and punctual.

MARGARET. Very punctual.

GRACE. Yes.

Slight pause.

Are you Margaret?

MARGARET. I am.

GRACE. Well… well…

She sits back down again on the stool.

I'm sorry.

She takes a handkerchief from her sleeve.

MARGARET. Are you not well?

GRACE. No. Yes. No I'm really, I am quite well. It's just that you look like… you resemble William… you do… you really do and… well, perhaps it's all a bit… a little… startling.

MARGARET. Startling?

GRACE. Yes.

MARGARET. You say you knew William?

In your note?

You sent a note.

GRACE. Yes, I did. And yes I knew William very well.

MARGARET. How?

GRACE. How?

MARGARET. Yes. How did you know William?

GRACE. Why we served together.

MARGARET. You served together?

GRACE. Yes.

Inniskilling Fusiliers.

MARGARET. William wasn't in the Inniskilling Fusiliers.

GRACE. No.

Yes. I know that.

MARGARET. William was in the King's Shropshire.

GRACE. Yes I know that.

    I was in the Inniskilling…

MARGARET. Lance Sergeant.

    William was a Lance Sergeant.

GRACE. Yes I know that.

MARGARET. So?

GRACE. So?

MARGARET. I'm afraid.

    This appears.

    You appear.

    This is all a little confusing, Miss Doherty.

GRACE. Is it?

MARGARET. Yes it is.

    And I am a busy woman.

    I have things to do.

GRACE. Of course you do.

MARGARET. I have to open the hall.

    I have to arrange… chairs.

    I have to…

GRACE. I brought some letters.

    Photographs.

MARGARET. I have all of William's letters.

GRACE. And a few locks of his hair.

    I promised, you see.

    I promised William that I would find you.

MARGARET. You promised William…?

GRACE. That I would find you.

MARGARET. It's hardly difficult to find me, Miss Doherty.

I was born and bred in Badgersbridge.

GRACE. As was William.

MARGARET. Yes. As was William.

GRACE. And he wanted to be buried here.

Did you know that?

Next to the railway station.

Under the old oak tree.

If anything happened.

He said that that was his spot.

MARGARET *is dumbfounded. She doesn't reply…*
GRACE *continues.*

He said that he would go missing there for hours, sketching the trains. Sketching the passengers.

He said that you used to love watching the trains too when you were little.

MARGARET. I didn't… I don't have time to watch trains.

GRACE. A peculiar pastime all right… but then William was…

MARGARET. William was what, Miss Doherty?

GRACE. A different sort.

MARGARET. A different sort, what do you mean by that, a different sort?!

GRACE. Well, he sketched everything, didn't he?

I have two of his notebooks from France.

Trucks, ditches, birds.

Tinned milk, satchels… and faces… so many faces.

And William could catch a face, couldn't he.

Couldn't he, Margaret...?

She makes to move toward her. MARGARET *flinches.*
GRACE *hesitates.*

He could catch the pain. The confusion... or the laughter.

William could catch everything.

See everything.

That's what made him different.

MARGARET. I have... I'm afraid I have no idea what you
mean?

GRACE. I brought them with me, Margaret.

William's notebooks.

I thought that I might bury them too but now I'm afraid that
I can't part with them.

MARGARET. Bury?

GRACE. Yes.

MARGARET. What on earth are you talking about, bury?

GRACE. I promised.

MARGARET. Promised who?

Promised what?

You are speaking in riddles.

GRACE. Promised William, of course!

But there was nothing left of him.

You know that don't you, Margaret?

They told you that didn't they – the army?

MARGARET. William died in action.

GRACE. Yes he did.

MARGARET. William died on the field.

GRACE. Yes.

Did they tell you how?

Did they tell you why?

MARGARET *doesn't answer.*

William was out with a posse laying roads.

He was laying a road in preparation for battle.

And we were behind the lines... that's the worst of it, Margaret... because he wasn't supposed to... we weren't supposed to die... because of the Balmorals.

But it was a stray shell.

A stray bloody shell.

They're not even sure if it was German or one of ours but it landed on top of him.

William.

It landed right on top...

And I wasn't there.

And I wish I was, Margaret.

Because I wish that I had died with him.

Because I don't know how to live.

How to live without him now.

Pause.

MARGARET *is aghast.*

Oh dear, have I said too much?

Have I said too much, Margaret?

MARGARET *sits down silently in a chair.*

I promised.

We promised, you see.

Me and William.

That if anything ever happened to either of us... that no matter what... we would bring the other home.

So William chose his tree, Margaret, and I chose mine.

And he told me exactly where it was, his tree, and I saw it as soon as I stepped off the train. I saw the ancient green of it. The thick of it.

But he also told me to find you.

'Find Margaret,' he said, 'you'll love Margaret.'

Slight pause.

So here I am.

MARGARET. Here you are.

GRACE. Yes.

MARGARET. 'Startling.'

There is a lot that is startling returns from this war.

Slight pause.

GRACE. So I thought... I hoped we might make a day of it?

MARGARET. Make a day of what?

Burying my brother?

GRACE. He said you had a sharp tongue on you all right.

But he also said to persevere... you're softer than you let on.

Slight pause.

MARGARET. William said that.

GRACE. Yes.

MARGARET. It certainly sounds like something he would say.

She pulls a hanky from her pocket.

What was that hymn you were playing?

GRACE. Hymn?

MARGARET. On the piano.

GRACE. Only 'Blighty'.

MARGARET. No, no before that?

GRACE. Oh. That was William's song for me.

MARGARET. Grace?

GRACE. Yes. I took the name after my mother.

Though I'm not so sure she'd enjoy the compliment...

MARGARET. I don't. I really don't understand this... You!

GRACE. Me?

MARGARET. Yes. I mean. Where... Where are you... your mother from?

GRACE. Kells.

Ireland.

MARGARET. Ireland?

GRACE. Yes.

MARGARET. Dear God...

GRACE. Don't you like Ireland?

MARGARET. I know nothing of it... Nothing, Miss Doherty, except that it is a heinous treasonous place.

GRACE. But what would give you that idea?

MARGARET. Your little Easter Rebellion!

You stabbed England in the back.

GRACE. Ahh...

Not everyone would see it that way.

MARGARET. Well, we see it that way.

We at Badgersbridge see it that way and we don't know any Irish, and William doesn't... didn't know any Irish!

GRACE. Thousands of us fought for you.

Thousands of us died.

MARGARET *cannot reply.*

So I need to finish, Margaret… or I need to start… I'm not
sure which.

But what I do know is that I have this little box… and it is
William… part of William, not the part that was blown to
bits… but the living part, the heart of him and I've kept it
with me for two years and I've kept it safe and now I need to
bury it… bury him under his tree… so that I can continue
with my life.

MARGARET (*exhales*). I see.

GRACE. Yes.

MARGARET. And you want me to be a part of this charade?

GRACE. Oh dear. You are hard.

The war has made you hard.

MARGARET. Life has made me hard, Miss Doherty.

This life.

GRACE. I don't doubt it.

I don't doubt that you have cause.

But we are survivors, aren't we?

Like it or not we survived.

And if we don't let in some light, Margaret.

Some love.

Or softness.

Then what was all the killing for?

Slight pause.

Now I would like you to be a part of this… this laying-down
of William.

Because William loved you.

He loved you with all his heart but...

MARGARET. I know that William loved me!

I know that...

GRACE. Good.

MARGARET. Good.

GRACE smiles.

GRACE. It's a cold corner, Margaret.

On that lonely road at Ypres.

I just want to fulfil my promise and bring William, my William... home.

MARGARET. Your William?

GRACE. Yes.

MARGARET. But aren't you a man, Grace?

GRACE. I'm a class of a man all right.

MARGARET. Dear God!

GRACE. Him again.

Slight pause.

MARGARET. I will ask you not to blaspheme...

GRACE. It's you that said his name, not me.

MARGARET. Oh... Oh you are clever. Clever!

I'll give you that.

GRACE (*sighing*). You are not the woman I imagined, Margaret.

MARGARET. And I must say... neither are you, *Grace Doherty*!

GRACE laughs now.

She really laughs.

GRACE. Grand.

Grand so.

I'll go.

I'll go and do this by myself.

MARGARET. No! No.

I… I… I want to know what you know.

I want to hear.

Hear.

What you have to say. Please…

GRACE. What I have to say?

MARGARET. Yes.

GRACE. I don't know what I have to say except that I love… loved your brother, Margaret.

MARGARET. Loved my brother?

GRACE. Yes.

MARGARET (*blurts*). I loved him too.

I… I loved him too.

Pause as MARGARET *attempts to pull herself together.*

Please.

God. Dear God…

GRACE. I'm sorry. I never meant to upset you.

MARGARET. I'm not…

I'm not upset. I just … I just need to verify.

GRACE. What?

MARGARET. That he. That you!

That you are what you say you are… William's friend?

GRACE. And how do you hope to do that?

MARGARET. Well, can I? May I start by seeing your face?

GRACE. My face?

MARGARET. Yes.

...please.

GRACE *pauses a moment then carefully lifts up her veil.*

MARGARET *looks at her. She reaches out her hand to* GRACE*'s face then pulls it back.*

Don't you get stopped?

Found out?

GRACE. Rarely in Soho.

MARGARET. Soho?

London?

Is that where you live?

GRACE. Yes, that's where I live.

MARGARET. But what about today on the train?

Did no one?

Did no one stop you?

GRACE. Today I am burying William.

I will not deny us.

MARGARET. Us?

GRACE. Yes. Us.

MARGARET. Well.

I think you are very brave, Grace Doherty.

GRACE. War can do that to you.

MARGARET. Can it?

I have a feeling that you were always brave.

Slight pause.

And did William?

Did William know how you felt about him?

GRACE. Oh yes. He loved me too.

MARGARET. God... (*Swallows the word now.*)

I can't pretend to understand it... what you are saying...
what I think you are saying.

GRACE. There's not so much to understand.

MARGARET. But I did...

I have heard ... about such things...

GRACE. Such things?

MARGARET *puts her hand to* GRACE*'s face again.*

This time she strokes it...

MARGARET. War is brutal.

GRACE. I know that.

MARGARET. War is cruel.

GRACE. I know that too.

MARGARET. And this war... this war, Miss Doherty... the
stories I have heard about life... life out there. I can't bear it.
I can't bear to think of William in it... all that mud and blood
and murder. William is... was, you see... the most gentle of
men. William wouldn't hurt a fly so I knew, I knew that he
would never survive it... as the truth came home... as the
truth, not their bloody lies of glory and victory and love of
country... but the truth... then I knew, I knew, William could
only die in it.

So I understand what you are saying, Grace, accept what you
are saying because I believe that so far away from home and
in times of great loneliness... one might ache... ache... for
any form of comfort...

GRACE. Why?

Are you lonely, Margaret?

MARGARET. I beg your pardon?

GRACE. Do you ache?

MARGARET. I... I! My. That is none of your business!

GRACE. Don't you have a sweetheart?

MARGARET. A sweetheart?

GRACE. Yes.

MARGARET *scoffs a laugh.*

MARGARET. The thought of it!

GRACE. So you still live with your mother?

MARGARET. No!

No.

Mother died.

GRACE. She died?

MARGARET. Yes.

Not long after William.

GRACE. Oh God, I am so sorry...

I didn't know.

MARGARET. How could you know?

What would you know about my mother?!

GRACE. Only what William told me.

And he spoke about her often... about you both often... and about your life here. He said it was a good life.

MARGARET. It was a good life.

Until Father died.

GRACE. Then there was no money.

MARGARET. How do you know these things?

GRACE. Because William…

> That's why he joined up, wasn't it, Margaret.

MARGARET. But we told him not to.

> We pleaded with him not to!

GRACE. He wanted to save you the house.

MARGARET. Ah yes, the house.

> The bloody house.
>
> As if we would have swapped William for a house!
>
> And we lost it anyway.
>
> Do you know that?
>
> Because Hunt only extended the lease to encourage William to join up. Once he died, William died, we were out on the side of the road. And Mother only lived three months after.

GRACE. Jesus!

MARGARET. Yes.

> A new family live there now.

GRACE. So where do you live?

MARGARET. I have been living… working in Birmingham.

> Until recently.

GRACE. In the city?

MARGARET. Yes.

GRACE. That's quite a change from Badgersbridge.

MARGARET. Yes, yes it is… it was.

> So William's sacrifice was useless.
>
> Utterly useless.

GRACE. Don't blame yourself.

MARGARET. I don't blame myself!

GRACE. They'd have got him eventually with conscription.

MARGARET. I suppose you are right.

Like they 'got' us all.

Pause.

Long pause.

GRACE. So what did you do in Birmingham, Margaret?

MARGARET. I worked.

GRACE. Worked where?

MARGARET. At Mills' Munition Factory. I looked after the accounts.

But now Mr Mills' nephew has returned from France so he will take up the position.

GRACE. Why?

MARGARET. Because…

It is his right.

GRACE. Is it?

MARGARET. Sorry?

GRACE. Is it his right?

MARGARET. I am not sure what you mean?

We must return, mustn't we?

We must return to what was before.

GRACE. Why?

MARGARET. Because the war is over.

GRACE. But it happened, Margaret.

MARGARET. I know it happened.

Don't we all know it bloody happened!

GRACE. So now everything has changed.

MARGARET. Not in Badgersbridge.

Never in Badgersbridge.

GRACE. So why don't you go back to Birmingham?

MARGARET. And live where?

I lost my lodgings when I lost my job, Grace.

I am now living back here with a relative.

And that is how your note found me.

GRACE. Lucky.

MARGARET. Lucky? I can assure you that there is nothing lucky about my situation.

GRACE. And you still haven't told me if you are lonely.

Slight pause.

MARGARET. I haven't told you because I haven't thought about it.

'*Lonely*'.

Lonely is a luxury for the likes of me.

GRACE. Why?

MARGARET. Because I cannot spare a thought for sentiment, Grace.

I cannot spare a thought for anything but my future, my circumstance. I cannot indulge in a fantasy of womanhood because, unlike you, I live it, I am forced to live it.

GRACE. Ah there it is again.

That sharp tongue.

MARGARET. Do you know what my options are, Grace?

What the options of a single woman are?

GRACE. No, I suppose I don't.

MARGARET. Of course not.

Well, when a woman has no family she has even less liberty. So for me… it is domestic service or marriage.

GRACE. That's it!?

MARGARET. Yes that's it. Despite my talents in business… which are numerous.

GRACE. I don't doubt it.

MARGARET. I am no longer permitted at the factory, Grace.

No longer required.

GRACE. And when you say business…?

MARGARET. I managed everything. Income, debtors, capital, expenditure, cash. Mr Mills used to praise me from the heights.

Mr Mills used to stand me in front of the workers once a month and tell them I was exemplary. I was his Wartime Home-time Hero.

And the business expanded during my time there… expanded three-fold and I never lost sight of a farthing, a farthing!

And I took meetings. Meetings with colleagues and other factory owners when Mr Mills was out. I was trusted entirely. Mr Mills said I could run the country if I wanted to but then the war ended.

And I… I, like all the women at the factory, was told that I was no longer needed, no longer employed.

GRACE. That's shite.

Now MARGARET *laughs.*

MARGARET. Oh… Oh you are funny.

Yes it is.

That is exactly what it is.

'*Shite*'.

She puts her hand over her mouth and laughs again.

GRACE *laughs too.*

GRACE. So I take it you liked Birmingham?

MARGARET. Liked? Liked Birmingham? I loved it! Why
wouldn't I? Dances, real dances... not the nonsense that they
call dances here... and pictures, Grace, they have a picture
house. And I used to dine at The Royal three nights a week
but now... now...

MARGARET *leans on the piano hitting a group of low notes.*

They both look at the piano.

Slight pause.

GRACE. Did William ever play this piano?

MARGARET. William?

GRACE. Yes.

MARGARET. Of course.

I'm sure... I'm sure he did...

GRACE. He taught me, you know.

Taught me all the notes.

MARGARET. Did he?

GRACE *sits on the piano stool and starts to play 'If You
Were the Only Girl in the World'.*

She speaks the next few lines over the music.

GRACE. He said I had an ear for it, a talent.

She plays some more.

A talent that saved my life.

She plays some more.

I'd like you to know, Margaret.

That it wasn't all horror.

For William.

It wasn't all '*mud and blood and murder*'.

There were happy days.

MARGARET. Happy days?

GRACE. Yes.

This song was one of our favourites.

William sang it.

MARGARET. William sang that?

GRACE. Yes.

GRACE *starts to sing 'If You Were the Only Girl in the World'*.

MARGARET *listens to the song*.

When GRACE *finishes:*

William was a standout, Margaret.

William was a star!

MARGARET. A star? A star of what?

GRACE. The Balmorals.

MARGARET. What are these Balmorals?

GRACE. The Balmorals were our family.

MARGARET. Are you deliberately being obtuse?

GRACE. Obtuse? I don't even know what it means.

MARGARET. Who were the Balmorals?

GRACE. They… We were a theatre troupe.

MARGARET. A theatre troupe on the Front?

GRACE. Of course.

MARGARET. That doesn't make any sense.

GRACE. Nothing makes sense, Margaret, if the war has taught us anything, it has taught us that.

She starts to play 'Take Me Back to Dear Old Blighty'.

MARGARET *enjoys it this time.*

GRACE *then switches midway to 'Hinky-Dinky Parlez-vous'… to her surprise* MARGARET *knows it and joins in.*

MARGARET. They used to sing that sometimes at the factory.

GRACE. Well now!

It seem you are a natural like your brother.

MARGARET. No I'm not.

GRACE. And beautiful!

MARGARET. I am not that either.

GRACE. Says who?

MARGARET *touches her hair.*

MARGARET. I see you can be charming as a man or a woman, Grace Doherty.

GRACE. I am only being honest.

GRACE *now touches* MARGARET *'s hair. There is a moment…*

MARGARET *pulls away.*

MARGARET. I am not sure I understand what you are telling me, Grace… about William?

William was a star?

GRACE. Yes, William was a star.

Everyone loved him.

We played as a duo mostly but sometimes he might take over…

GRACE *starts to play 'There's a Long Long Trail A-Winding'.*

When he sang this you could hear the war medals rattle because even the most hardened old fart had to reach for his hanky… the whole hall would be struggling to hold back the tears.

MARGARET. But where did he play?

GRACE. In the canteen or depot.

In the rest camps or hospitals...

Wherever there were soldiers, Margaret, there were Balmorals.

MARGARET. I can't believe it.

There was singing on the Front?

GRACE. Of course.

And dancing and play-acting.

To bring some relief from the carnage.

MARGARET. But did the army know about it?

GRACE. The army organised it... eventually.

Shakespeare is good for morale, don't you know.

And penny operas and bawdy jokes and pantos...

GRACE *switches from the previous melodic number now to something familiar like 'It's a Long Way to Tipperary'. She keeps playing the piano as they speak.*

Anything to take them away... take us away...

MARGARET. But William never showed any interest in theatrics before?

GRACE. Didn't he?

MARGARET. No! Never!

GRACE. He was that good that they used to swap him between battalions to stop him getting killed. They used to swap us both. Because we were worth more singing, Margaret, than firing any guns.

MARGARET. But William did get killed.

GRACE *stops playing.*

GRACE. Yes, William did get killed.

And the singing was never the same after.

Not for me anyway.

MARGARET. I knew nothing of this.

How did I know nothing of this?

GRACE. Because it doesn't quite fit the picture, does it.

Singing for King and Country?

But they needed us, Margaret… them Tommys and Freddies and Alberts… they needed the Balmorals as much as they needed air. Soldiers would sit in the tent for hours, you know, before curtain-up.

I can still hear them, you know, in my dreams.

I can still hear them stamp and clap and ROAR!

And I can hear them laugh, laugh and laugh like little children trying to convince us to keep going because if we could pretend then so could they.

And I can hear their hearts burst, Margaret, when we sing.

Because I could feel their longing every night on that stage.

I could feel it in my bones.

When I would stick my head out of a cardboard window on a cardboard-cut-out train and they might all sing with me –

Birmingham… Leeds or Manchester…

And their longing would hang in the air.

And their terror would scream through their cheers.

And their ache would rattle.

Because they knew, Margaret.

They knew they were never going home.

Pause.

Long pause.

The memory hangs in the air.

Do you play at all?

MARGARET. No. No. I never learned.

GRACE. Pity.

I might have had a job for you.

MARGARET. A job for me?

GRACE. I was thinking of putting a troupe together.

MARGARET. A troupe?

GRACE. To tour.

MARGARET. Tour where?

GRACE. I don't know. Music halls?

Village halls?

She smiles.

There are a few of the old Balmorals made it home.

MARGARET. Goodness, I think that's a great idea!

GRACE. Do you?

MARGARET. People need a lift.

People need something different.

GRACE. They do.

It's the one thing I miss about home... the singing.

MARGARET. Ireland?

GRACE. Yeah.

MARGARET. Will you go back there?

GRACE. God no, I don't think they'd know what to make of me now... in Kells!

'Tis far from fine pianos I was reared.

MARGARET. This is hardly a 'fine' piano, Grace.

GRACE. I dunno…

She plays a few notes again.

She plays, doesn't she?

But I was thinking, I might need someone to manage us?

MARGARET. Manage you?

GRACE. Do the accounts.

Book the tours.

MARGARET. What are you saying?

GRACE. I am saying… I am saying that I grew up on a farm, Margaret, not even a farm, more like a scrap of land beyond a forgotten town… and I was even useless at that. Useless at digging. Useless with the cattle so I don't know how to do much… I don't know how to make a living now if I don't sing. And these things… managing… accounts… they are not my talents.

MARGARET. I'm sure there must be scores of theatrical managers in London?

GRACE. I'm sure there are.

It was just an idea.

MARGARET. What was just an idea?

GRACE. That you might join us?

MARGARET. Join you?

A theatre troupe?

GRACE. Yes.

MARGARET. But I've never been to the theatre in my life.

GRACE. Why not?

MARGARET. My mother would never allow it!

William would never allow it!

GRACE. Ah… I think William might have changed his mind.

MARGARET. But I couldn't… I wouldn't dream of it!

GRACE. Why not?

MARGARET. Because… because it's immoral… isn't it?

Theatre?

GRACE. Immoral? Really?

What gave you that idea?

GRACE *starts to play 'It's a Long Way to Tipperary' (the dirty version).*

(*Sings.*) That's the wrong way to tickle Mary…

MARGARET. Are you serious?

GRACE *stops playing.*

GRACE. Yes I'm serious.

There's no need for marriage or domestic service, Margaret, if you come with me and do the accounts.

MARGARET. Oh God… why didn't you… why didn't you come here weeks ago?

GRACE. I was busy getting home from France.

MARGARET. But now it's too late…

GRACE. Why?

MARGARET. Because I said I'd marry Geoffrey!

GRACE. Geoffrey?

Who the hell is Geoffrey?

MARGARET. Geoffrey is Mr Mills' son.

GRACE. The one who took your job?

MARGARET. No, that's his nephew.

Geoffrey is his son and Mr Mills wants me to marry him.

GRACE. Mr Mills wants you to marry Geoffrey?

MARGARET. Because Geoffrey isn't quite himself.

GRACE. What does that mean?

MARGARET. It means that he fought at Estaires.

Geoffrey fought at Estaires.

And he came home a shadow of himself.

A half of himself, Grace.

A blind blithering mess if I'm honest.

GRACE. Estaires?

MARGARET. His skin… it hangs in strips.

And his limbs jerk…

And he screams, oh God he screams, Grace.

At all the horrors lurking behind his bandages.

But Mr Mills said he might improve, would improve with the right care.

With love.

With a wife.

GRACE. If Geoffrey fought at Estaires, Geoffrey was hit by gas, he won't improve, Margaret, don't marry him.

What Geoffrey needs is a nurse, not a wife.

MARGARET. I'm not sure that Mr Mills knows the difference.

GRACE. So tell Mr Mills thanks but no thanks.

MARGARET. I can't.

I can't disrespect that sacrifice, can I?

Geoffrey's sacrifice?

GRACE. What about your sacrifice?

Your brother.

Your home.

And now Mr Mills has even taken your job.

You owe the bastard nothing.

He's just looking for cheap labour.

Or he probably has his eye on you himself.

She winces.

I'm right, aren't I?

Slight pause.

MARGARET. You are not wrong.

GRACE. I knew it.

They're all the same, toffs.

Don't throw yourself away, Margaret.

You're too good for them.

And you've survived this far.

We've survived this far.

So fuck the lot of them.

MARGARET. But what will they think of me?

How would I hold my head up?

GRACE. Hold your head up where?

If you come with me to Soho, no one will judge you there.

MARGARET. Soho?

GRACE. Yes.

MARGARET. Soho.

GRACE. Where there are dances, real dances, Margaret… and theatre and picture houses.

MARGARET. And what would… what would be my remuneration?

GRACE. Ah that's more like it!

Your remuneration can be whatever you like!

And if we make a go of it, I'll make you a partner, how about that?

You'd have your own business then, Margaret, and no one could tell you you were 'no longer required'.

MARGARET. My own business.

GRACE. And your own life!

The Immoral Balmorals, why not?

MARGARET. Why not… because there must be more, mustn't there?

There must be more to this life than duty?

I mean, isn't it duty that started all this?

Duty and fear?

'If England Falls, You Fall.'

And I tell you it makes me sick.

GRACE. That's the girl…

MARGARET. It makes me sick what they asked of us.

What they took from us.

From you and Geoffrey and William… and me.

And for what?

For what, Grace?

GRACE. So that they could hold on to their estates.

So that they could hold on to Ireland, and their factories, and their money, but they don't know what they've started, Margaret, I'm telling you… they don't know what they've started.

Don't marry Geoffrey.

Whatever you do.

It will be a life sentence.

MARGARET. I know.

Don't you think I know that!

I just don't know that I have any choice.

GRACE *holds her gaze*.

GRACE. I'm giving you a choice.

Come with me.

MARGARET. Come with you?

GRACE. Manage the troupe.

Do the accounts.

MARGARET. I could, you know.

I could…

GRACE. I know you could… of course you could… and if it makes it any easier you can marry me.

MARGARET. Marry you?

GRACE. Then I can live my life and you can live yours.

MARGARET. Dear God.

GRACE. You can bring him too if you like.

He might like Soho.

MARGARET *laughs*.

All I ask is that you let me be myself.

Let me be Grace.

MARGARET *looks at* GRACE.

MARGARET. That's… that's not so difficult.

GRACE. So you like me?

MARGARET. I could grow to like you.

GRACE. That'll do.

   Slight pause.

MARGARET. But can I ask you one thing?

GRACE. Anything.

MARGARET. Why?

   Why the clothes?

   GRACE *looks down at her clothes, smoothing the line of her skirt.*

   Is it Irish?

   GRACE *guffaws.*

   Please don't laugh at me.

GRACE. Sorry. Sorry, Margaret but no, no… it's not Irish.

   My poor sisters didn't even have a decent dress between them let alone me.

   No.

   It was later.

   The clothes came later.

   In France.

MARGARET. Why?

GRACE. Because… because there is such a comfort in it.

   Isn't there?

   In the frills and the lace and the softness.

   Such softness!

   Like a soft day.

   Cottons and silks.

   It felt.

   It feels.

   It feels like something beyond, Margaret.

MARGARET. Beyond what?

GRACE. All this.

All the '*mud… and blood… and murder*'.

Slight pause.

MARGARET. Soft?

Like a mother?

GRACE. Perhaps.

MARGARET. Like a lover?

GRACE. Just soft, Margaret.

And in a world of killing men.

In a world of scattered limbs.

Scattered fury.

'Soft' feels like heaven.

MARGARET. And now?

GRACE. Now 'soft' is just a part of who I am.

Farmboy.

Singer.

Killer.

Grace.

Slight pause.

So will you come with me, do you think?

MARGARET. Do you know, Grace Doherty.

I might.

I just might.

Slight pause.

Though I can hear my mother turn in her grave.

GRACE. Hah! But not William!

William is only dusting off his shoes.

So that he can dance with us.

MARGARET. Dance?

Why? Are we going to dance?

GRACE. Why not?

GRACE *starts to play a little ragtime music now on the piano*.

MARGARET *lights up*.

MARGARET. What's that?

GRACE. Ragime. It's from America.

MARGARET. From America!

GRACE. Your brother loved it.

MARGARET. Have you ever been to America?

GRACE. Not yet.

We'll go.

We'll both go!

The lights change and the music fills the hall.

GRACE *leaves the piano and takes* MARGARET *in her arms*.

They start to dance 'The Castle Walk' (it is a fun, fast dance).

MARGARET. Wooooh! Did you and William dance like that?

GRACE. Yes we did.

MARGARET. It's WILD!

GRACE. Yes it is.

MARGARET. I'm beginning to believe that William really did send you here.

GRACE. Only beginning?

MARGARET. Like a guardian angel.

Do you have guardian angels in Ireland?

GRACE. Millions of the Hoors!

MARGARET laughs.

You laugh like him too.

MARGARET. Do I?

GRACE. Deep and honest.

Slight pause.

I wonder, do you waltz like him?

MARGARET. I don't know.

GRACE. Will we try?

MARGARET. Yes please.

GRACE clicks her fingers and a slow waltz starts to play.

She and MARGARET waltz.

Shall we go and bury William after?

GRACE. Would you like to?

MARGARET. Yes.

Yes, I think…

I think that might be lovely, Grace Doherty.

MARGARET puts her head on GRACE's shoulder.

They continue to dance.

The lights fade.

Interval.

ACT TWO

SEAN DOHERTY *is in his mother's living room. It is old-world Victorian with piano and high windows. There are theatrical pictures on the piano.*

SEAN *is in his pyjamas rooting through piles of papers.*

He takes a sip from his mug.

The doorbell rings. He looks at his watch.

SEAN. Shit!

> *He leaves to answer the door, returning quickly with* MIRJANA BEKTO, *who wears a blue nurse-like uniform.*

I was just looking through papers... trying to find your number... Tabitha Home Care right!?

MIRJANA. No. I am with The Nightingales.

SEAN. Oh yes The Nightingales, of course.

I'm sorry.

I think Tabitha were tomorrow.

MIRJANA. Very good.

SEAN. Again I'm so... I'm terribly sorry.

I told her!

I told Mother that you would be here by ten.

I can't imagine where she's disappeared to!

MIRJANA. I see.

SEAN. She didn't leave a note, a message but I presume... I'm presuming... I'm hoping that she's just popped out.

MIRJANA. So you said.

SEAN. To the shop.

   To the chemist.

   Something like that.

MIRJANA. Yes.

SEAN. Yes.

MIRJANA. Did you try telephoning her?

   Does she use a mobile?

SEAN. Oh yes. Incessantly!

   But no, I mean yes, I tried it… I've been trying it for hours…
   no, not hours, since I noticed that she… since I got up.

MIRJANA. And she didn't answer?

SEAN. No.

   She didn't answer.

MIRJANA. Is that a cause for concern?

SEAN. Unfortunately no.

   I don't mean unfortunately… I don't mean I'd like to be
   concerned. What I mean is that I know Mother and she
   doesn't answer when she doesn't want to.

MIRJANA. Ah, I see.

SEAN. Yes.

   Slight pause.

MIRJANA. So you would like me to wait, Mr Doherty?

SEAN. Yes. Yes please.

   If you don't.

   If you don't mind…?

MIRJANA. I don't mind.

   It simply depends on how long?

SEAN. Of course.

Of course.

I can understand that.

MIRJANA. Good.

SEAN. Thank you. Thank you, Miss – ?

MIRJANA. Bekto.

SEAN. Thank you. I'm sorry about... about all this... as you can see I'm a tad stressed... it's all a bit of a stress... Mother!

MIRJANA. Is it?

SEAN. Oh yes... she's not... she's not quite cooperating.

She's not quite accepting growing old.

MIRJANA. I see.

SEAN. In complete denial actually... if I'm honest.

MIRJANA. Right.

SEAN. Until she falls... then... panic stations!

MIRJANA. Does she fall?

SEAN. Yes she falls a lot.

MIRJANA. Is there an underlying condition?

SEAN. Belligerence!

He laughs, MIRJANA *doesn't.*

No, sorry... what I mean is it's hard to know what's going on really, she won't go to a doctor... she believes in herbs... holistic... holistics... but this is the second time I've had to come home this year because of a fall. I don't live here, you see, don't live in the UK. Haven't for years.

I'm in Luxembourg.

MIRJANA. I see.

SEAN. I teach at the university there.

Classics.

MIRJANA. Very good.

SEAN. Thank you.

MIRJANA. Yes.

SEAN. Have you been to Luxembourg?

MIRJANA. No...

SEAN. Oh, well, it's beautiful... on the river... old-world, I like it... I'm happy... well, relatively... I was until... until... well, lots of stuff but God here I am 'going on'. I do go on, apologies about that. Cindy says it's nerves... she says I'm nervous but I think it's she that makes me nervous... sorry, Cindy is my wife... ex-wife... about-to-be ex-wife.

MIRJANA. I see.

SEAN. So I'm going through a divorce right now as well as Mother!

MIRJANA. Right.

SEAN. But you don't want to hear about that.

You're not here to hear about that.

MIRJANA. No.

SEAN. No.

Sorry. Apologies.

MIRJANA. No problem.

So Mum is on her own, is she?

SEAN. Yes, Mum is on her own.

And that's a worry now... it never was before...

MIRJANA. How old is Mum?

SEAN. Eighty-two, she's eighty-two.

MIRJANA. Eighty-two.

SEAN. And she's starting to have these little crises.

MIRJANA. Crises?

SEAN. When she can't find things... or when she falls... or when something goes wrong in the house. So I need to... I really feel I need to put something... some care in place for her.

MIRJANA. Of course.

SEAN. I mean, the neighbours are good but it's not fair to expect... you know... and there are new families now, of course, on the street, as is to be expected, many of Mother's old friends are gone.

MIRJANA. Yes.

SEAN. So now she telephones me when there's a problem. Daily. Or on the hour sometimes. And then she might forget she's on the phone because something distracts her, one of the cats distracts her and I'm left... I'm left holding... and worrying...

MIRJANA. I see.

SEAN. And I don't have anyone to call... here... not any more... because they've all died... her crew... her gang... or they live abroad... and I can't just come running.

Keep come running.

Because I've got a career to think of.

MIRJANA. Of course.

SEAN. Would you?

Would you like to sit down?

While you're waiting?

MIRJANA. Sit down?

SEAN. Yes, I find it a tad nerve-racking having you stand... standing there.

MIRJANA. Nerve-racking?

SEAN. I'm just... it might be more comfortable to sit.

MIRJANA. Okay, we will sit.

SEAN. Wonderful.

He takes a breath.

Sorry if I appear, if I appear a bit...

MIRJANA. Stressed.

SEAN. Do I?

MIRJANA. It is natural.

SEAN. Is it?

MIRJANA. Of course.

SEAN. Oh... okay... good.

And can I offer you some tea?

MIRJANA. No thank you.

SEAN. Coffee?

MIRJANA. No thank you.

SEAN. Vodka?

MIRJANA. No thank you.

She hesitates. He laughs.

SEAN. Only joking!

It's only ten o'clock in the morning!

MIRJANA. Yes it is. It is only ten o'clock in the morning.

He smiles, as he eyes the bottle of vodka on top of the piano.

He sits on the piano stool.

SEAN. So. Miss Beeko, perhaps we should have a chat about your services... Tabitha services as you are here.

MIRJANA. Nightingales.

SEAN. Oh yes, of course.

MIRJANA. Well we actually believe it is important to have the client present at the first meeting.

SEAN. Do you?

MIRJANA. Yes.

SEAN. Well she will be, she should be… any minute now… but it would be great to get some sense of what you do?

MIRJANA. That really depends on the client.

SEAN. Does it?

MIRJANA. Ageing is a very individual journey.

SEAN. Indeed.

MIRJANA. At Nightingales we create a package to suit the client's individual needs.

SEAN. Well, that sounds good…

MIRJANA. Yes.

SEAN. So you call every day?

MIRJANA. If that is what is required.

If that is what the client needs.

SEAN. And you do dinners?

Clean the house?

MIRJANA. We don't clean.

We care, Mr Doherty.

SEAN. Right. So I should organise a cleaner or something separately should I?

MIRJANA. If a cleaner is required.

SEAN. Right.

MIRJANA. But it is really best to discuss all of the options when the client is present

SEAN. I know, yes… I got all that… it's just that Mother… well, she is not exactly thrilled at the prospect of a carer, Miss Beeko, she rather guards her independence.

MIRJANA. I understand.

SEAN. Do you?

MIRJANA. Of course.

SEAN. Well, that's a relief… so how do we bring her around to the idea?

MIRJANA. She would need to be here?

SEAN. Ha! Haha… yes, she would need to be here.

That would help, wouldn't it!

MIRJANA. That would help very much.

SEAN. Right.

Got it…

MIRJANA. Perhaps you could telephone your mother again?

SEAN. Perhaps I could.

He dials the number. He smiles at MIRJANA. *Gets voicemail. Hits speaker and we hear a sprightly elderly voice say: 'You have reached the telephone of Willemina Doherty. I am afraid I am not available to take your call at present as I am hopefully doing something far more interesting! Leave a message if you dare! Byeeeee!'*

And we hear the beep.

That's her.

That's Mother.

MIRJANA. Interesting.

SEAN. Oh yes, she is that.

MIRJANA. Do you think, Mr Doherty, that your mum might have made herself unavailable on purpose?

SEAN. I think that might be a distinct possibility.

As I said… she won't accept that she is getting on.

And I've tried to tell her, tried to explain… that I can't drop everything… that I can't –

MIRJANA. Keep come running.

SEAN. Exactly! Because it's...

MIRJANA. Quite a distance...

SEAN. Indeed.

But she reacts... you know.

Mother...

She can be... she IS quite dramatic.

MIRJANA. Is she?

SEAN. She comes from a theatrical background.

MIRJANA. I see.

SEAN. Worked as a theatrical agent for years. She represented some of the greats... Hopkins, Hancock, Caine...

He waits for a response, there is none.

They would be quite famous around here?

MIRJANA. I know.

SEAN. Anyway it all means that Mother is quite the performer. She likes to quote Plath... or Virginia Woolf...

They're poets.

MIRJANA. I know who they are.

SEAN. And sometimes she likes to put her head in the oven.

In a kind of ode to Plath.

To get her way.

She does it on Skype.

I mean, when I'm on Skype.

When she Skypes me...

And wants me to come home.

It's not...

She's not an easy woman, Miss Beeko.

MIRJANA. Bekto.

SEAN. Sorry.

You'll have to forgive me.

I'm just, I'm not quite myself.

I'm going through a divorce.

Did I tell you that?

As well as Mother!

MIRJANA. Yes you told me that.

SEAN. Ah!

MIRJANA. Yes.

Pause.

SEAN. I'm actually quite conscious, Miss Bee… Bekto that I'm still in my pyjamas.

MIRJANA *doesn't reply.*

I'd like to.

If you don't mind. I'd like to just hop up and change.

I won't… I really won't be a minute.

He is gone. MIRJANA *is left alone. She sighs.*

She starts to look around a bit.

She looks at the photos on the piano.

She tidies the papers on the lid. Then she lifts them off the lid.

She looks around. She can't help herself. She lifts the lid and hits a few notes, beginning to play…

SEAN *returns smartly dressed.*

Oh!

You play?

MIRJANA. No. No.

SEAN. It sounds like you play?

MIRJANA. I used to.

SEAN. Really?

Why did you stop?

MIRJANA. I stopped because… life changed.

SEAN. Did it?

MIRJANA. Yes.

Pause as she offers nothing more.

SEAN. Well, I suppose life changes.

MIRJANA. Yes it does.

SEAN. Are you sure you won't have a coffee?

MIRJANA. No. No thank you.

SEAN. I'll try Mother again in a minute.

MIRJANA. Very good.

Slight pause.

SEAN. You're not from here, are you?

MIRJANA. Pardon?

SEAN. You're not from Birmingham?

MIRJANA. No.

I am from Badgersbridge.

It is a village twenty-two miles from…

SEAN. Badgersbridge! I know Badgersbridge!

MIRJANA. Do you?

SEAN. Yes. That's where my grandmother was from.

Mother's mother!

Oh my God she'll love that.

Mother will love that.

MIRJANA. It is a coincidence.

SEAN. Isn't it!

So how long have you been in Badgersbridge?

MIRJANA. I…

She pauses.

Twelve years.

SEAN. But what on earth brought you out there… there's nothing in it?

MIRJANA (*hesitates*). My… my husband.

SEAN. Really? He's from there?

MIRJANA. Yes he is.

SEAN. And what's his name?

MIRJANA. Sorry?

SEAN. His name?

MIRJANA. His name is Tom.

SEAN. Tom?

MIRJANA. Yes.

SEAN. Well… that's… super…

Slight pause.

MIRJANA. I'm afraid I cannot wait the entire morning, Mr Doherty.

SEAN. Oh?

No.

Of course not.

MIRJANA. It might be best for us to arrange another time?

When your mother is here.

SEAN. Certainly… if… if you think that's best.

MIRJANA. I do.

Suddenly his mobile phone rings.

SEAN. Ah!... that might be her... that might be Mother!

I'll just... I'll answer...

He hops up with the phone to his ear

Mother!

Oh thank God, where are you?... I have the lady... the lovely lady from the help-people here and you won't believe it, she's from Badgersbridge! (*Nods enthusiastically at* MIRJANA.) Her name? Bekto but... no, not originally... she lives... what? What do you mean you're at the airport?... You're joking. Where? You're going Where? But... but you agreed to this... to meet her! No, it's not okay... it's absolutely not okay... who's meeting you over there? Frankie? I can't believe it. I can't believe you're doing this. No I will not mind the cats. No. No. I'm due back to class next week, you know that. I have PhD students... This is unbelievable... I'm not... I'm absolutely not shouting! Don't... don't do, Mother... don't hang up this phone.

He looks at MIRJANA.

She hung up.

She's gone to Barcelona.

MIRJANA. Barcelona?

SEAN. For the opera.

MIRJANA. I see.

SEAN. Bloody hell. Do you see? Do you see what I have to put up with?!

'Mind the cats.'

I bet that's what this whole thing is about.

Get me home to mind the cats.

He puts his head in his hands.

I'm sorry. I am so terribly sorry, Miss Bekto, to waste your time like this.

MIRJANA. It's fine.

SEAN. It's not fine. It is absolutely not fine. And I don't know what I'm going to do about it?

He reaches for the vodka and pours it into his coffee cup.

MIRJANA. I'm not sure that that will help.

SEAN. No. I know.

But I'm at the end of my tether with her… I'm telling you.

MIRJANA. How about I call, I call again, Mr Doherty, on your mother's return?

SEAN. Okay.

MIRJANA. And we can arrange a suitable package?

SEAN. Okay.

MIRJANA. It will put your mind at rest.

SEAN. Will it?

I'm not sure I remember how that feels… to be at rest.

He takes a slug of the vodka.

MIRJANA *hesitates.*

She stands.

I mean, there's a part of me thinks it is marvellous that she travels… still travels… not that she ever comes to Luxembourg, mind you… *'Too bureaucratic' – 'dull'.* But at eighty-two she can be quite forgetful, quite confused and that would make her vulnerable, don't you think?

MIRJANA. I think that depends on the person, Mr Doherty…

SEAN. And then I think that 'the day she stops is the day she drops'.

MIRJANA. Yes –

SEAN. And that I'm just a bloody nuisance, bloody fussing… but then, there's a call or a fall and I hear the quake in her voice and I know, I know that she's not as '*sure*' as she'd like to pretend, that she's not as '*strong*'... and then I worry, I worry, Miss Bekto, because I love her...

Slight pause.

She's my mother.

MIRJANA. Yes.

SEAN. And despite... well, despite everything... I don't want anything to happen to her... I feel responsible.

MIRJANA. Of course.

SEAN. Particularly as there are just the two of us.

MIRJANA. I see.

SEAN. So I think it is vital, vital, that I put something in place this time... whether she can agree with me or not... do you think... do you think that that's possible? Do you think that I am right?

MIRJANA. I think, certainly, from what you say, that there is a need for services.

SEAN. Excellent.

MIRJANA. But we must be respectful.

SEAN. Of course.

MIRJANA. Your mother must be allowed to play her part...

SEAN. So do you?... could you?... do you think you might have some advice?

She hesitates.

MIRJANA. Well.

Do we need to worry about Mother in Barcelona, is she travelling alone?

SEAN. She says she'll stay with Frankie.

MIRJANA. Is Frankie a relative?

SEAN. No.

Frankie is an old friend. One of the last still on his feet.

He used to sing at the Liceu.

MIRJANA. I see.

SEAN. You say that a lot: 'I see.'

MIRJANA. Do I?

SEAN. Yes.

MIRJANA. I see.

She smiles for the first time.

SEAN *smiles* (*wracked but encouraged*).

She sits.

SEAN. Thank you, I really appreciate this…

MIRJANA. I will just… ask a few questions.

SEAN. Please do…

MIRJANA. To build a picture.

SEAN. Excellent…

MIRJANA *takes a blue folder and pen from her bag.*

So how did you get into all this?

MIRJANA. Pardon?

SEAN. Home-care? How did you get into it?

MIRJANA. I studied.

SEAN. I see…!

He laughs awkwardly. She doesn't.

MIRJANA. I worked as a carer for ten years.

Then I became a supervisor.

SEAN. Congratulations.

MIRJANA. Pardon?

SEAN. On the promotion.

It was a promotion, I presume?

MIRJANA. Yes, it was a promotion.

SEAN. Very good.

Well done.

MIRJANA. Thank you.

Now, I will ask you some more questions, for the form.

SEAN. Do. Please do.

MIRJANA. Are there any other siblings?

SEAN. No.

She ticks the box.

That's the problem, a problem you see... there's really no one else.

MIRJANA. No husband or partner?

SEAN. No.

She ticks the box.

Mother is a bit of a solo-run. I never met my father. She didn't seem to think that that was important, despite my ardent pleas.

MIRJANA. I see –

SEAN. We lived with Gran and Gracie, here, until they died. Then it was just the two of us, and that's when the chaos started.

MIRJANA. Okay –

SEAN. Mother used to drag me with her you see, wherever the work took her, Tokyo, LA, New York. I rarely attended shool. I was to be her little protégé. But unfortunately I had no interest... in the business, in theatre, and also I had no talent so that was a disappointment. I was a disappointment because I look quite like Gracie apparently but could never quite live up to her.

MIRJANA. Gracie?

SEAN. My grandfather.

MIRJANA....I see!

SEAN. You'll hardly get all of that into that little box?

MIRJANA. No.

SEAN. Cindy is right, isn't she?

   I do go on!

MIRJANA. It is not a problem.

SEAN. Thankfully one of Mother's friends finally convinced her to let me go to boarding school.

MIRJANA. Ah...

SEAN. And I loved it.

   The peace of it.

   Bedtimes.

   Dinners.

   Rules!

MIRJANA. Good.

SEAN. I have always thrived on routine.

MIRJANA. Excellent...

   She is about to ask her next question.

SEAN. So where did you grow up yourself?

MIRJANA. Me?

SEAN. Yes.

MIRJANA. I am not sure that that is important.

SEAN. I think it is... if... if you don't mind?

MIRJANA. No... I don't mind. It is just...

SEAN. Poland?

MIRJANA. No.

SEAN. Croatia?

MIRJANA. No. Sarajevo.

I grew up in Sarajevo.

SEAN. Bosnia!

MIRJANA. Yes.

SEAN. That's amazing!

MIRJANA. Is it?

SEAN. I was just at a concert, Dino Merlin, before I came over.

MIRJANA. Dino Merlin?

SEAN. He's a singer.

MIRJANA. Yes I know that he is a singer.

SEAN. And I'm a big fan.

MIRJANA. Okay –

SEAN. Don't you like music?

MIRJANA. Of course I like music...

It is just that it is not so important, Mr Doherty.

SEAN. There's no box for that then?

MIRJANA. No.

SEAN. No box for music?

MIRJANA. No.

SEAN. Maybe we ask all the wrong questions?

Slight pause.

MIRJANA. Maybe.

Maybe we do.

Slight pause.

SEAN. So did you meet your husband in Sarajevo?

MIRJANA. No!

SEAN. You met him here?

MIRJANA. Yes I met him here…!

SEAN. Were you on holiday?

MIRJANA. No!

>…I am living here. I was living here.

>We lived here since 1996.

SEAN. Really?

MIRJANA. Yes.

SEAN. Yet you still have your accent.

MIRJANA. I am still the same person.

SEAN. And who is that?

MIRJANA. Pardon?

SEAN. I'd just… I'd like to know your name, your first name, if you didn't… if…

MIRJANA. Mirjana.

SEAN. Mirjana?

MIRJANA. Yes.

SEAN. And does it mean anything?

>I find that your Balkan names often mean something?

MIRJANA. Do you?

SEAN. Yes. We have a lot of Eastern European students.

MIRJANA. Oh…

SEAN. They're terrific.

>Highly motivated.

MIRJANA. I see.

SEAN. So does it mean anything?

MIRJANA. It means… *Star of the Sea*.

SEAN. That's lovely.

MIRJANA. Thank you.

Slight pause.

SEAN. And I'm Sean.

It doesn't mean anything. It's Irish.

MIRJANA. I see.

Sean.

SEAN. Yes.

I like the way you say it.

MIRJANA. Why?

SEAN. I don't know. It sound strong.

Sounds Balkan, when you say it.

MIRJANA. And what is Balkan?

SEAN. Carved out of the rock.

MIRJANA. Really?

SEAN. Yes.

MIRJANA. And have you ever been to Bosnia?

SEAN. No.

But I think I can see it in your eyes.

Pause.

She looks back to her form.

MIRJANA. Can Mother wash herself?

Can she dress?

SEAN. Yes and Yes.

MIRJANA. How is her appetite?

SEAN. I don't know, if I'm honest.

It used to be voracious.

Now there's not that much in the fridge.

MIRJANA. I see.

SEAN. Is that bad?

MIRJANA. I don't know.

I will have to weigh her when we have our first appointment.

SEAN. Excellent.

He watches her write.

So tell me all about Badgersbridge, Mirjana?

MIRJANA. Badgersbridge?

There is not so much to tell.

SEAN. I still can't believe you live there.

Do you know my grandparents actually met in the village hall? That's the story anyway, at the end of the war.

Is it still there? The hall?

MIRJANA. Yes it is still there.

SEAN. Imagine!

MIRJANA. I teach dance there on a Saturday morning.

SEAN. Do you?

MIRJANA. Yes.

SEAN. Dance!

MIRJANA. Yes.

SEAN. That's amazing!

MIRJANA. Again?

SEAN. I dance!

I love to dance!

Ballroom.

MIRJANA. I see.

SEAN. Myself and Cindy.

That's how we met!

MIRJANA. Okay –

SEAN. And that's the bitch of it, you know.

We're still dancing partners.

Because we're good. Very good.

Not champions now or anything… but BDSF members and we've won a few competitions.

MIRJANA. Very good…

SEAN. But… it's becoming really difficult with the divorce…

MIRJANA. I'm sure.

SEAN. Because she's vital, Cindy, really vital and passionate and fast… on the floor that is. Not in life, no, in life she's not passionate, not any more…

MIRJANA. Right.

SEAN. Is that too much information?

MIRJANA. Perhaps…

SEAN. Because in life she has become unreachable… kind of somewhere behind the door.

I'm speaking metaphorically, of course.

MIRJANA. Of course.

SEAN. And are you – ? Is your – ? Are you happy?

MIRJANA. Am I happy?

SEAN. Yes.

MIRJANA. Happy how?

SEAN. With your husband, with Tom?

MIRJANA *shifts.*

MIRJANA. Ah, with Tom.

SEAN. Yes.

MIRJANA. Tom lives in London.

SEAN. Not in Badgersbridge?

MIRJANA. No. Not in Badgersbridge.

We have two daughters.

SEAN. Oh you do?

MIRJANA. Yes.

SEAN. Don't they miss Tom?

MIRJANA. He comes home on weekends.

He stays with his mother.

SEAN. Ah…

MIRJANA. Yes.

Slight pause. MIRJANA *looks back to her folder.*

Only one or two more questions, Mr Doherty.

SEAN. Sean.

She looks up.

MIRJANA. Sean.

He smiles.

SEAN. What kind of dance do you teach?

MIRJANA. Pardon?

SEAN. In the village hall?

MIRJANA. I teach… ballet.

SEAN. Fantastic.

Did you study ballet?

MIRJANA. Yes I did. At the Academy of Belgrade.

SEAN. Wow.

MIRJANA. And then with a Mrs Parker in Digbeth.

SEAN. Oh dear... I hope Mrs Parker wasn't a come-down.

MIRJANA. I'm afraid she was.

But I still loved, love to dance.

SEAN. Of course.

MIRJANA. I teach children at the hall.

The committee give it to me for very little, because it is usually empty.

SEAN. Is it?

MIRJANA. Yes. It is in need of some repair.

SEAN. What a shame.

MIRJANA. Yes.

MIRJANA. I have...

I am helping the village to fundraise.

SEAN. Really?

MIRJANA. They are all quite... elderly, on the committee, quite... traditional.

SEAN. I can imagine.

MIRJANA. And what they don't realise is that there are grants. Council grants. Heritage grants. For which we can apply.

SEAN. Marvellous.

MIRJANA. To fix the roof and to...

Restore...

SEAN. Of course.

MIRJANA. You just need to be good with forms.

She lifts up her pen.

I am very good with forms.

SEAN. Well, I hope they know how lucky they are to have you.

Out there in Badgersbridge.

MIRJANA. We will see.

SEAN. Do you know...

I think that's where Gran and Gracie had their first dance!

MIRJANA. Gran and Gracie?

SEAN. My grandparents. In the village hall. Yes, I'm sure of it.

Good God! There ought to be a plaque!

They danced 'The Castle Walk'.

MIRJANA. 'The Castle Walk'?

SEAN. It's a ragtime number.

MIRJANA. I know what it is.

SEAN. Hang on...

SEAN sits down to the piano, hurling whatever is left on top to the floor and starts to play the tune... it takes a while until he finds it... he talks over his attempts at the right notes.

Gran is the reason I love dancing. She was my partner in crime. We used to dance here, right here in this living room. Ragtime. It helped with her sciatica. Nothing like a good stretch, she said. Poor Gran, she had absolutely no flair... left that all to Gracie... but she was a stickler for the steps... what was it?... yes...

He leaves the piano stool once he gets going and the music continues without him, just like in Act One.

He starts to dance something like 'The Castle Walk' steps.

MIRJANA. I'm afraid that is not 'The Castle Walk'.

SEAN. Yes it is.

MIRJANA. No. No. It is forward – back.

SEAN. Forward what?

MIRJANA. Here, I'll show you.

She takes his hand and starts the dance… she is leading… they get it… they get faster and faster… they finish, they have really enjoyed it.

Did you really dance like that with your grandmother?

SEAN. Yes. And I only came up to her chest!

Had to dodge each bosom on the swing!

MIRJANA *smiles*.

Gosh, I haven't thought about that for years.

Good old Gran. Everything made sense when she was around.

But I could only hold on to her till I was nine, you see.

Because Gracie died and Gran ached.

I have never seen such grief.

I think she wanted to die herself so that she could join them, William and Grace.

It took less than a year…

He smiles.

MIRJANA. You still think about her?

SEAN. All the time.

She was more of a mother than Mother…

He does a few steps again, smiling as he remembers MARGARET.

MIRJANA. You should come visit.

SEAN. Visit?

MIRJANA. The hall… where your grandmother… where they met.

SEAN. Do you know I'd love that.

MIRJANA. Good.

MIRJANA smooths her skirt.

She picks up her folder and pen.

SEAN. I'd love it.

She smiles.

MIRJANA. Good.

SEAN. Have you family here yourself?

Other family? Other than Tom?

MIRJANA. Why?

SEAN. Just curious.

MIRJANA. No.

I don't have other family.

SEAN. You came here alone then?

From Sarajevo?

MIRJANA. No.

I came with my mother.

But she never… she never settled here.

She has returned.

SEAN. That must be lonely?

MIRJANA. Lonely?

I don't think so.

I have never thought about it – *lonely.*

SEAN. Do you go back yourself?

MIRJANA. No.

SEAN. Never?

MIRJANA. No.

SEAN. Why is that?

MIRJANA. Because I am busy. Because I work and I have the girls, my girls and they live a good life, that is what is important… that is what is important to me.

SEAN. Of course.

I'm glad.

MIRJANA. Thank you.

SEAN. And how old are they… how old are your girls?

MIRJANA. They are six and eight years old.

SEAN. Still small.

MIRJANA. Yes… still… small.

SEAN. What a shame for your mother to miss them?

MIRJANA. Yes.

Yes.

But that is her choice.

She chooses the past.

SEAN. The past?

How?

MIRJANA. I…

She shifts a little.

I am not sure we should be having this conversation…

SEAN. Why not?

MIRJANA. Because I am at work.

Because I have other appointments, Sean.

SEAN. But I just…

MIRJANA. I really don't talk…

SEAN. Why not?

MIRJANA. Because no one is interested…

SEAN. I'm interested!

I'm interested…

Slight pause.

Why did she… why did your mother go back?

MIRJANA. Because she waits.

She waits for my brother.

Davud.

He went missing.

He was political.

He went missing in '94.

SEAN. Oh God…

MIRJANA. Him too!

God also went missing, Sean.

From Sarajevo.

SEAN. You were there in the war!

MIRJANA. Of course.

Of course I was there in the war.

SEAN. Of course. Oh dear, Mirjana… how awful. I mean,
I could never! I can never quite understand what happened…

MIRJANA. I am not sure that anyone can understand…

SEAN. And it all happened so fast.

MIRJANA. Yes it did.

It happened fast.

SEAN. Nationalism, wasn't it?

After the the death of Tito?

MIRJANA. All of that...

And none of that.

Some collective madness.

I don't know.

I don't know, Sean.

I was only a girl...

SEAN. I remember the terrible images on television.

MIRJANA. And I remember them outside my window...

SEAN. Of course...

MIRJANA. I remember... I remember... that one day we were living... having dinner... like any ordinary family... in any ordinary city... eating peas... and the next... Chaos!

SEAN. Really...

MIRJANA. War comes quickly, in my experience.

And when it comes it devours everything...

SEAN. I cannot imagine.

MIRJANA. No, you cannot imagine, Sean.

Because you have always been safe here.

And that safety is a gift.

But it seems to me that in England you don't treasure it.

In England you will only know it when it is lost.

SEAN. Gosh...

MIRJANA. I will never go back.

SEAN. I'm so sorry.

MIRJANA. Why?

It was not your war.

And it was not mine.

SEAN. So how did you get out?

MIRJANA. Our home was… our home was destroyed.

And we were in a camp.

Myself and my mother.

A UN camp.

They settled us here…

SEAN. In Digbeth?

MIRJANA. Yes, in Digbeth.

She smiles.

My Nirvana!

He smiles.

SEAN. And were there others?

From your family?

MIRJANA. No.

I… We…

We were the only two to survive.

SEAN. God!

MIRJANA. My father…

And my sister…

SEAN. Oh no…

MIRJANA. I'm afraid… Yes.

SEAN. That's dreadful… God.

MIRJANA. She used to sit on the front step you see, my sister.

The front step of our apartment.

To meet her friends.

Because ours was the side of the street that still caught
a little sunshine.

Farah, that was her name.

Farah meaning joy.

And she and her friends would meet.

They would meet and smoke and kiss on our front step –
despite the snipers, despite our parents' warnings. Because...
because the chaos was their world now... our world...
our normal.

And I used to watch them from my window.

Farah Bekto.

Sixteen.

And I used to wish that I was her.

So beautiful and so cool.

Because I didn't have her beauty.

And I didn't have her fashionable friends.

Slight pause.

But death was never far away in Sarajevo.

And when you are young you believe that you can dance
through it... escape it.

You believe you are invincible.

Don't you?

Unbreakable.

And who wants to live in a basement when you are young?

Who wants to live in fear?

So she embraced it...

We all embraced it.

The carnage.

And we tried to live.

Just live.

And it was such a beautiful night when Farah died.

Such a warm night.

I remember watching her.

Two of her friends were playing guitar.

They were singing 'Stairway to Heaven'.

They used to sing that song to taunt the aerial bombers.

And I watched them.

I watched them flirting.

Laughing.

But then I heard it… heard the mortar.

So I left the window and I timed myself turning down the stairs.

Two by two by two.

Not scared.

Not knowing.

Because mortars were normal now in Sarajevo.

Mortars filled the sky like stars.

They came.

They always came.

But we always escaped.

We could time our escape.

It might seem hard to understand, Sean, but when you are in a war you begin to know… instinctively… just when a bomber is close… and just how many minutes you have to run… Just how many minutes…

So I don't know what happened that night.

I don't know how Farah got it wrong…

Maybe they had some beer down there on the steps.

Or maybe they were just having too much fun.

But her clock.

Farah's inner wartime clock.

Was seconds out.

She was…

They were…

Blown to pieces…

Pause.

SEAN *is speechless.*

That is why I like the quiet of Badgersbridge.

That is why I will never go back.

I live.

I live only for my daughters.

Farah and Grace.

So they will know nothing.

They will never know… that chaos.

They both sit in silence.

MIRJANA *touches a key on the piano.*

She starts to play 'Stairway to Heaven'.

She plays the song.

When she finishes, she closes the lid and rubs her hand gently over it.

I no longer own a piano.

I miss it.

She stands up.

I must return to work now, Sean.

You will call us when your mother returns?

SEAN. Of course.

I will.

Certainly.

MIRJANA. It was nice to meet you.

She smiles.

She turns to leave.

SEAN. And nice... incredible... incredibly nice to meet you, Mirjana.

MIRJANA. Very good.

SEAN. And I might... I might... just... pop over... if that's.

If that's still on offer.?

To visit the village hall?

MIRJANA. Of course.

SEAN. Of course?

MIRJANA. I think.

I think that might be lovely... Sean Doherty.

SEAN. Oh good...

The lights fade.

End.

A Nick Hern Book

Crossings first published in Great Britain in 2018 as a paperback original by Nick Hern Books Limited, The Glasshouse, 49a Goldhawk Road, London W12 8QP, in association with Pentabus Theatre Company and New Perspectives

Crossings © 2018 Deirdre Kinahan

Deirdre Kinahan has asserted her moral right to be identified as the author of this work

Cover design by Stephen Long

Designed and typeset by Nick Hern Books, London
Printed in Great Britain by Mimeo Ltd, Huntingdon, Cambridgeshire PE29 6XX

A CIP catalogue record for this book is available from the British Library

ISBN 978 1 84842 805 8